BASIC OF COMMODITIES MARKET

DEEPAK SHINDE

COPY RIGHT 2016 by Deepak Shinde

All the right reserved .No part of this book may be reproduced or transmitted in any form, or by any means electronic or mechanical including photocopying, recording or any information storage without permission, in writing from publisher..

First edition in 2014

Published by Deepak Shinde

Book on

Basic of commodities market
The target of success

BY

DEEPAK SHINDE

Index

S no	Topic	Page
Chapter 1	THE BASIC OF MARKET	3
Chapter 2	Exchange Traded Funds (ETFs)	11
Chapter 3	Fundamental of commodities	23
Chapter 4	Technical of Commodities Investing	28
Chapter 5	Commodity futures and option	36
Chapter 6	Top traded commodities	49
Chapter 7	Terminology	66

Chapter 1

THE BASIC OF MARKET

1.1 A commodity market

A commodity market is a market that trades in primary economic sector rather than manufactured products. Soft commodities are agricultural products such as wheat, coffee, cocoa and sugar. Hard commodities are mined, such as gold and oil. Investors access about 50 major commodity markets worldwide with purely financial transactions increasingly outnumbering physical trades in which goods are delivered. Futures contracts are the oldest way of investing in commodities. Futures are secured by physical assets. Commodity markets can include physical trading and derivatives trading using spot prices, forwards, futures, and options on futures. Farmers have used a simple form of derivative trading in the commodity market for centuries for price risk management.

A financial derivative is a financial instrument whose value is derived from a commodity termed an underlie .Derivatives are either exchange-traded or over-the-counter (OTC). An increasing number of derivatives are traded via clearing houses some with Central Counterparty Clearing, which provide clearing and settlement services on a futures exchange, as well as off-exchange in the OTC market

Derivatives such as futures contracts, Swaps (1970s-), Exchange-traded Commodities (ETC) (2003-), forward contracts have become the primary trading instruments in commodity markets. Futures are traded on regulated commodities exchanges. Over-the-counter (OTC) contracts are *"privately negotiated bilateral contracts entered into between the contracting parties directly".*

Exchange-traded funds (ETFs) began to feature commodities in 2003. Gold ETFs are based on "electronic gold" that does not entail the ownership of physical bullion, with its added costs of insurance and storage in repositories such as the London bullion market. According to the World Gold Council, ETFs allow investors to be exposed to the gold market without the risk of price volatility associated with gold as a physical commodity.

1.2 What is the 'Commodity Market?'

A commodity market is a physical or virtual marketplace for buying, selling and trading raw or primary products, and there are currently about 50 major commodity markets worldwide that facilitate investment trade in approximately 100 primary commodities.

Commodities are split into two types: hard and soft commodities. Hard commodities are typically natural resources that must be mined or extracted (such as gold, rubber and oil), whereas soft commodities are agricultural products or livestock (such as corn, wheat, coffee, sugar, soybeans and pork).

1.3 Major Commodity Exchanges

The major exchanges in the United States, which trade commodities, are domiciled in Chicago and New York with several exchanges in other locations within the country.

The Chicago Board of Trade (CBOT) was established in Chicago in 1848. Commodities traded on the CBOT include corn, gold, silver, soybeans, wheat, oats, rice and ethanol. The Chicago Mercantile Exchange (CME) trades commodities such as milk, butter, feeder cattle, cattle, pork bellies, lumber and lean hogs.

The New York Board of Trade (NYBOT) commodities include coffee, cocoa, orange juice, sugar and ethanol trading on its exchange. The New York Mercantile Exchange (NYMEX) trades commodities on its exchange such as oil, gold, silver, copper, aluminum, palladium, platinum, heating oil, propane and electricity.

Key commodity markets in regional centers include the Kansas City Board of Trade (KCBT) and the Minneapolis Grain Exchange (MGE). These exchanges are primarily focused on agriculture commodities. The London Metal Exchange and Tokyo Commodity Exchange are prominent international commodity exchanges.

Commodities are predominantly traded electronically; however, several U.S. exchanges still use the open outcry method. Commodity trading conducted outside the operation of the exchanges is referred to as the over-the-counter (OTC) market.

1.4 Regulation of Commodity Markets

In the United States, the Commodity Futures Trading Commission (CFTC) regulates commodity futures and options markets. The CFTC's objective is to promote competitive, efficient and transparent markets that help protect consumers from fraud, manipulation and unscrupulous practices. Regulation of commodity markets have continued to remain in the spotlight after four leading investment banks were caught up in a precious metals manipulation probe in 2014.

1.5 Commodity price index

A **commodity price index** is a fixed-weight index or (weighted) average of selected commodity prices, which may be based on spot or futures prices. It is designed to be representative of the broad commodity asset class or a specific subset of commodities, such as energy or metals. It is an index that tracks a basket of commodities to measure their performance. These indexes are often traded on exchanges, allowing investors to gain easier access to commodities without having to enter the futures market. The value of these indexes fluctuates based on their underlying commodities, and this value can be traded on an exchange in much the same way as stock index futures.

Investors can choose to obtain a passive exposure to these commodity price indices through a total return swap or a commodity index fund. The advantages of a passive commodity index exposure include negative *correlation with other asset classes such as equities and bonds, as well as protection against inflation. The disadvantages include a negative yield roll due to continuo in certain commodities, although this can be reduced by active management techniques, such as reducing the weights of certain constituents (e.g. precious and base metals) in the index.*

The first such index was the CRB ("Commodity Research Bureau") Index, which began in 1958. Due to its construction it was not useful as an investment index. The first practically investable commodity futures index was the Goldman Sachs Commodity Index, created in 1991 and known as the "GSCI". The next was the Dow Jones AIG Commodity Index. It differed from the GSCI primarily in the weights allocated to each commodity. The DJ AIG had mechanisms to periodically limit the weight of any one commodity and to remove commodities whose weights became too small. After AIG's financial problems in 2008 the Index rights were sold to UBS and it is now known as the DJUBS index. Other commodity indices include the Reuters / CRB index (which is the old CRB Index re-structured in 2005) and the Rogers Index.

In 2005 Gary Gorton (then of Wharton) and Geert Rounwehorst (of Yale) published "Facts and Fantasies About Commodities Futures", which pointed out relationships between a commodities index and the stock market, and inflation. They were both employed as consultants to AIG Financial Products (AIG-FP), which was responsible for managing the DJAIG Index. Gorton's other role was to provide AIG-FP with the mathematical modeling expertise underpinning the construction of "Super-Senior" credit derivatives linked to mortgage-backed securities so as to ensure AIG was not exposed to risk of loss.

1.6 Categories

The constituents in a commodity price index can be broadly grouped into the following categories:

- *Energy (such as Coal, Crude Oil, Ethanol, Gas Oil, Gasoline, Heating Oil, Natural Gas, Propane)*
- *Metals*
    - *base metals(such as Lead, Zinc, Nickel, Copper)*

- - Precious metals (such as Gold, Silver, Platinum, Palladium)
- Agriculture
  - Grains (such as Cocoa, Corn, Oats, Rice, Soybeans, Wheat)
  - Softs (such as Sugar, Butter, Cotton, Milk, Orange Juice)
  - Livestock (such as Hogs, Live Cattle, Pork Bellies, Feeder Cattle)

Indexes

- World Bank Commodity Price Index
- Continuous Commodity Index (CCI)
- Summer Haven Dynamic Commodity Index
- Asthma Commodity Index (AMCI)
- Commin Commodity Index
- Dow Jones-UBS Commodity Index
- Goldman Sachs Commodity Index
- Thomson Reuters/Jefferies CRB Index
- Rogers International Commodity Index
- Standard & Poor's Commodity Index
- NCDEX Commodity Index
- Deutsche Bank Liquid Commodity Index (DBLCI)
- Credit Suisse Commodity Benchmark Index (CSCB)
- UBS Bloomberg Constant Maturity Commodity Index (CMCI)

- Merrill Lynch Commodity index eXtra (MLCX)
-

1.7 commodity index fund

A commodity index fund is a fund whose assets are invested in financial instruments based on or linked to a commodity price index. In just about every case the index is in fact a commodity futures index.

ou cannot invest in an index, but you can invest in a fund. A Commodity Index Fund is a fund which either buys and sells futures to replicate the performance of the index, or sometimes enters into swaps with investment banks who themselves then trade the futures. The biggest and best known such fund is the Pimco Real Return Strategy Fund. There are many other funds, such as:

Oppenheimer

iShares S&P GSCI Commodity Indexes Fund

Barclays [

JP Morgan (1994)

These are very different from, and should not be confused with, commodity funds that hold real assets (oil refineries, farms, forests etc.) such as:

Chase Physical Commodity Index

Bear Stearns

Chapter 2

Exchange Traded Funds (ETFs)

Exchange Traded Funds (ETFs)

2.1 Introduction

Exchange Traded Funds (ETFs) continue to generate extensive media coverage. This is a growing asset management and banking segment which simultaneously provides implementation tools to institutional investors and fund alternatives for the retail investor. This paper looks at what ETFs are and how they work. It goes on to examine potential uses for institutional investors as well as highlighting some disadvantages. We finish with some comment on recent product developments including issues around counterparty credit risk.

2.2 What are ETFs?

In terms of legal entity, ETFs are generally established as open-ended collective investment schemes which are then listed on one or more stock exchanges. In the eyes of the retail investor, they are perhaps best thought of as a mutual fund/stock hybrid. ETFs typically combine the *investment management proposition of an index-tracking mutual fund with the trading characteristics of the shares of a listed company.*

- *In the eyes of the institutional investor however, they are perhaps better thought of as an investment trust/unit trust hybrid. Many investors buy and sell shares in the ETF on-exchange as though they were an investment trust, and intra-day they are 'closed ended' funds. However, investment trusts typically trade at a discount to net asset value because of uncertainty as to whether there will be a willing buyer at the time an investor wishes to sell. To remove this discount, ETFs act like 'open ended' mutual funds (tradable once a day, at net asset value plus or minus dealing costs) but only to a select group of institutions. This group — called 'authorized participants' or 'market participants' — has an arbitrage opportunity should the ETF trade away from net asset value intra-day.*

- *In recent years, product offerings have extended beyond funds to exchange traded products where the underlying legal entity is a bond. This is the way in which most commodity exchange traded products are structured. Some providers are also launching active products within ETF structures, but it is a nascent sector at this stage of market development, and we have focused on passive exposures here.*

2.3 Sources of return

Generally, both single commodity and index-tracking ETCs track a total-return index, meaning there are three sources of return (it is critical that the precise details of individual products are inspected before investing):

The change in price of the future – largely affected by changes in the spot commodity price

The roll – as the front month future is 'rolled' into the near month, there is usually a price difference between the two, which is reflected in the price of the ETC

Interest on collateral – since futures are margined instruments, interest is earned on the cash value of the initial investment

2.4 Benefits and features

The benefits of commodities investment are well known: they bring balance to a portfolio, can be used as an inflation hedge, have low correlation to equities and bonds which, according to modern portfolio theory, should result in reduced risk without necessarily reducing returns.

ETCs are one of several vehicles which can be used to gain commodities exposure, and the table below sets out the relative merits of this innovative product.

Features

➢ Low tracking error

– the open-ended nature of these securities ensures tracking error is minimized and creates an arbitrage opportunity should the price drift away from the NAV

- Open-ended

Price not subject to supply and demand forces

- Liquid

ETCs are open-ended and can be created on demand. Additionally, market makers are committed to provide on-book liquidity all day

- Traded and settled on a regulated exchange, the

Same as any share

Familiarity, regulated, no mandate barrier, protection of CCP, settles T+3* through Euro clear

UK & Ireland Limited (formerly CRESTCo)

- No management of physical or futures positions

Hassle-free – reduces back-office costs

- Ability to go long or short

Potential for positive returns in bull and bear markets Lendable and marginable

➢ *flexibility*

Potential to recoup management fee through lending

➢ Market access

All types of investors can gain exposure and are charged the same fees

➢ Transparency

No hidden fees, accurate pricing

Who are they for?

ETCs are very flexible products and can be used by all types of investors for a number of different purposes: whether you are an institutional investor looking for liquid, quick and easy commodity exposure during London hours; a hedge fund manager with a view on a commodity sub-index; a private wealth manager with clients crying out for exposure to 'alternatives'; or a private investor looking to participate in commodity markets using an existing

Stockbroker account, ETCs are redefining commodities trading for all types of investors.

2.5 How do ETFs work?

Figure 01 shows the mechanics of an ETF. Most investors buy and sell ETF shares in the secondary market via a broker on the relevant exchange. These trades settle just like any normal equity trade on exchange. Away from this normal dealing activity and all but invisible to most investors is the primary market in the ETF, where designated authorized participants can create (buy) or redeem (sell) ETF shares in return for the basket of underlying assets that makes up the index being tracked. This creation-redemption process takes place once a day after the market closes and is typically offered by ETF sponsors with a minimum order size of around US$5 million.

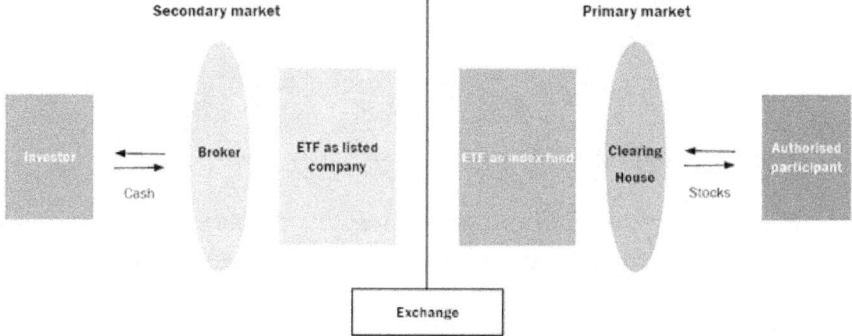

The investment management of the assets underlying the ETF (the index-tracking fund) either follows the same process as other forms of index fund management (generally full replication of index constituents) or uses total return index swaps. In either case, the existence of both long and short holders of the ETF shares means that sponsors usually aim for lower tracking errors than is often the case in similar institutional index funds.

To access ETFs, institutional investors will need the operational capability and the regulatory permission to instruct a broker to trade the ETF shares and a custodian to settle that trade. This means that many pension funds will access ETFs via an existing investment manager.

2.6 Industry players

For any ETF to work effectively requires a four-way partnership:

- ETF sponsors who own the fund legal entity and are responsible for fiduciary oversight of the fund and for marketing. Usually they also provide investment management of the underlying assets though this can be outsourced.

- Authorized participants are either brokers interested in executing large creation-redemption trades or specialists who act to provide continuous liquidity in an ETF across multiple exchanges.

- Stock exchanges.

- Index providers.

2.7 Products available

The ETF industry continues to see growth in numbers of funds and assets under management. At the end of July 2011 there were over 2,800 different ETFs with combined assets of US$1.4 trillion traded across 51 different stock exchanges globally.

The landscape is very different from ten years ago when there were just 202 ETFs and assets totaled US$105 billion. [1] Judging by the number of filings for new funds, this trend looks set to continue. At the time of writing there are 816 new ETF fund prospectus filings at the SEC in the US alone. [2]

"ETFs typically combine the investment management proposition of an index-tracking mutual fund with the trading characteristics of the shares of a listed company."

2.8 Target customers

One of the notable things about ETFs is their ability to appeal simultaneously to retail and institutional investors. Institutional investors and hedge funds, drawn by the large range of asset classes in exchange-tradable form provide scale and liquidity to many ETFs which, in turn, reduce trading costs to the retail investor.

The different customer types targeted by ETF sponsors are:

- High net worth individuals, wealth managers and private banks; the most important channel in Europe among established ETF sponsors.
- Asset managers using ETFs for short-term trading (as an alternative to futures) or for completion strategies (in asset classes or sectors where the manager lacks expertise).
- Institutional funds, particularly those with an in-house investment management function, will use ETFs in transition management.
- Hedge funds have found ETFs attractive for both long and short exposures. When shorting, ETFs on less liquid underlying assets (for example, emerging market equities or high yield debt) have the advantage of combining exposure to less developed markets with the operational framework of a developed market equity.
- Retail investors consider ETFs as an alternative to mutual funds or direct equity investment.
- Defined contribution investors have been relatively slow to take up ETFs despite some obvious attractions. Often this is because of DC operational platforms which are built around mutual funds (in the US) or insurance products (in Europe). These platforms struggle to value and settle ETFs which trade throughout the day rather than at the once-a-day valuation point favored by pension providers.

2.9 Liquidity

One of the main attractions of ETFs is their tradability. Through a number of different market environments over the last few years, including periods of heightened volatility, ETFs have continued to exhibit high levels of liquidity. This has held across different asset class exposures and generally includes smaller funds where some commentators have expressed concern over likely liquidity. High liquidity is due to brokers having at least two sources: the liquidity of the ETF shares themselves as well as that of the underlying constituents. Thus, trading costs in an ETF are frequently lower than the weighted average of costs of trading the index constituents being tracked.

2.10 Uses for institutional investors

We now turn to the uses to which ETFs can be put by institutional investors (and their investment managers). Some of these are relatively simple strategies where ETFs are one of a number of candidate implementation vehicles. Others are more complex and rely on the specific characteristics of the ETF.

- **Short-term liquidity management.** The tradability of ETFs across a wide range of underlying asset classes mean they are a viable alternative to futures for cash-flow management purposes.

- **Asset allocation implementation.** ETFs were initially conceived as implementation vehicles for tactical or dynamic asset allocation.

- **New beta exposure.** The growing array of asset classes and benchmarks upon which ETFs are created has made them a useful way of making an initial allocation to a new asset class. There are two reasons for this: the underlying portfolio construction gives clarity to the nature of the investment and the exchange listing provides the ability to trade new asset exposures using the well understood operational infrastructure of developed market equities.

- **Transition management.** If a fund knows that it wants to change asset allocation or manager but is unsure of the precise make-up of the new target stock portfolio, then an ETF can be used in transition to buy time for the fund. A quick transition can be made into the relevant asset class ETF and then at a later date, when the new target portfolio is determined, a combination of the ETF's in-specie redemption and program trading can be used to deliver that specific stock portfolio.

- **Long-short exposures and portable alpha.** ETFs can also present opportunities when used on the short side by investors with appropriate governance, operations and risk systems. One example might be hedging part of the beta exposure in a less liquid asset class while enjoying a higher than normal allocation to the skill offering of an active manager in that asset class.

"There are many additional uses for ETFs that can be considered by funds depending on their objectives and expertise."

2.11 Disadvantages

ETFs do, though, come with a number of disadvantages. For institutional funds in particular, the ETF Total Expense Ratio may well cover a number of product features that the investor does not often need — for example, branding and intra-day liquidity. For this reason, it is usually the case that institutions looking for longer-term exposures to an index mandate will find better value for money among more traditional institutional pooled index funds rather than ETFs. Tax considerations should also play their part in ETF selection. Investors need to satisfy themselves of the tax efficiency of holding a particular ETF rather than the underlying assets or an alternative pooled vehicle.
Another potential disadvantage comes from the obvious product proliferation in the ETF segment. This will make it increasingly difficult for time-poor investors to distinguish between useful innovation and fad.

Counterparty risk issues

There has been a certain amount of commentary recently about counterparty risk embedded in ETFs following the publication of a number of adverse reports on the issue from regulators. [3] These concerns relate to both swap based (or synthetic) ETFs and to the securities lending practices within more traditional stock based ETFs.

Counterparty risk in swap-based ETFs arises from both the swaps that are used to get index-tracking performance and the management of collateral. Risk is heightened by the possibility that the ETF sponsor, swap provider and selector of collateral could be the same financial institution; a position that might give rise to conflicts of interest in times of market stress.

We would stress the importance of potential ETF investors taking time to understand the capital structures inside these funds and the risk controls put in place by the sponsor. Although broad guidelines are contained in the fund prospectus, transparency of practice is still not high. This is a disadvantage of an ETF structure where the end investor has little choice about participating in securities lending or swaps.

Secondly, we would argue that as securities lending or swaps involve the end investor taking on additional counterparty credit risk, they should receive some compensation for taking that risk. It remains unclear whether existing ETF structures offer sufficient compensation for credit risk in the current market environment. This is perhaps the biggest weakness of ETFs today. The nature of securities lending for example, is that the rewards are shared between manager and investor but the distribution of risk in a default scenario is less clear given a lack of case law in the area. Therefore, ETF investors probably have little choice other than to assume that they are taking the vast majority of any counterparty credit risk involved and should weigh this when deciding whether or not to invest in an ETF.

2.12 New products

There continues to be a large new product pipeline in the ETF segment. Many of these are from new entrants looking to develop distribution. Of more interest to institutional investors will be those new funds which deliver genuine investment innovation. There are two areas to highlight here.

- **New betas.** We have written elsewhere on the attraction of new beta exposure and specifically non-price weighted indices. [4] We are beginning to see this concept appear in ETF wrappers with the launch of minimum variance equity products being a good example. [5]

- **Fixed income ETFs.** These have been available for a number of years but we would suggest that institutions have not yet fully exploited the liquidity and transparency offered by on-exchange equity market trading mechanisms brought to bear on exposure to over-the-counter bond investments.

"There are many additional uses for ETFs that can be considered by funds depending on their objectivity and expertise."

Conclusion

ETF growth is set to continue as the number of funds and users rise. They offer a number of implementation applications to institutional investors, some as an alternative to derivatives and others which rely on their unique trading infrastructure. We believe that product extensions into new betas and deeper into fixed income may offer future possibilities. However, for longer-term holdings investors may find better value for money in institutional index fund products and all ETF users need to evaluate the counterparty credit risks inherent in current structures.

Chapter 3

Fundamental of commodities

3.1 Investment

Thinking Ahead

This article is written by members of our Thinking Ahead Group (TAG) who are part of Investment at Towers Watson. Their role is to identify and develop new investment thinking and opportunities not naturally covered under mainstream research. They seek to encourage new ways of seeing the investment.

Fundamental analysis is a means of analyzing commodities and trying to predict where the prices of commodities should be trading and what they will do in the future. The main basis for fundamental analysis is supply and demand.

Supply and demand is a very simple equation, but it gets more complicated when you try to forecast prices in the future. Commodities trade in cycles. Sometimes supplies will be tight and prices will be high.

Other times, we just have too much of a commodity and prices fall accordingly. I like to look at commodities that are trading at multi-year highs or lows. Eventually, the picture will change and that will lead to a good trading opportunity.

Price movements in commodities using fundamental analysis can be broken down into these simple formulas:

- Demand > Supply = Higher Prices
- Supply > Demand = Lower Prices

3.2 Supply of Commodities

The supply of a commodity is the amount that is carried over from previous year(s) of production and the amount that is being produced during the current year. For example, the current supplies of soybeans would include the amount of crops in the ground and the amount that is left over from the previous season. Typically, the more that is carried over from the previous season, the lower the prices will fall.

There are many factors that can impact the supply of commodities like weather, amount of acres planted, production strikes, crop diseases and technology.

The main thing to remember when using fundamental analysis is that high prices for commodities will lead to an increase in production, as it is more profitable to produce commodities when prices are higher. As you might expect, demand will typically drop as prices move higher.

3.3 Demands for Commodities

Demand for commodities is the amount that is consumed at a given price level.

The rule of thumb is that demand will increase when the price of a commodity moves lower. Oppositely, demand will decrease as the price of a commodity increases. There is an old saying among commodity traders that low prices cure low prices. This means that more of a commodity will be consumed at lower prices, which lowers the supply and thus prices will eventually increase.

Just think about how you would use more gasoline at $1.50 per gallon than you would at $3 per gallon. Fundamental analysis of commodities is simple economics. Consumption patterns change as the prices of commodities move higher and lower.

3.4 Using Fundamental Analysis to Predict Future Prices of Commodities

Prices will fluctuate in the short term, so it is not easy to make fundamental forecasts of commodities prices and make short-term trades. It is even more difficult for new commodity traders to do this. I recommend that new traders, and even experienced traders, use a long-term strategy when using fundamental analysis to forecast commodity prices.

You should look for trends that are developing that will cause a shift supply and demand factors.

To begin your fundamental research of commodities, there are numerous reports that are compiled by government sources – USDA, Department of Energy and the Futures Exchanges. Many of the larger commodity brokers will also publish fundamental research for their clients.

It may seem like a daunting task to find all the current data and compare it to previous years and see how prices reacted under those conditions. Worse yet, you have to forecast in the future as to what the supply and demand scenario will be. I can tell you it is almost impossible to do this, especially since you will be competing against experts who have a lot more information and experience than you.

What you want to do is look for trends in production and consumption and trade with that bias. For example, if the supplies of corn are at a five-year high and we just planted a record amount of acres of corn for this season, it is likely that corn futures will trade with a downward bias. You would be likely want to trade from the short side.

Now, at some point, the price of corn will get too low and demand will increase. Or, there might be weather problems during the growing season that will lower the production of corn. In these cases you have to be flexible and realize that prices won't go down forever.

The longer-term trends in commodities are easier to spot with fundamental analysis, but I prefer to use technical analysis to capture shorter-term movements in commodities prices. Most professional commodity traders like to know what the big picture is with commodities using fundamental analysis and then they use technical analysis to time their entries and exits.

A commodity futures contract is a commitment to make or accept delivery of a specified quantity and quality of a commodity during a specific month in the future date at a price agreed upon when the commitment is made.

Commodities traded in the commodity exchanges are required to be delivered at the contracted price, ignoring all the changes in the market prices. Both the participants (Buyers & Sellers) are allowed to liquidate their respective positions by way of cash settlement of price between the contracted and liquidated price, no later than the last trading session of the specified expiry date.

3.4 Commodities exchange

A commodities exchange is an exchange where various commodities and derivatives are traded. Most commodity markets across the world trade in agricultural products and other raw materials (like wheat, barley, sugar, maize, cotton, cocoa coffee, milk products, pork bellies, oil, metals, etc.) and contracts based on them. These contracts can include spot prices, forwards, futures and options on futures. Other sophisticated products may include interest rates, environmental instruments, swaps, or freight contracts.

Commodities exchanges usually trade futures contracts on commodities, such as trading contracts to receive something, say corn, in a certain month. A farmer raising corn can sell a future contract on his corn, which will not be harvested for several months, and guarantee the price he will be paid when he delivers; a breakfast cereal producer buys the contract now and guarantees the price will not go up when it is delivered. This protects the farmer from price drops and the buyer from price rises.

Speculators and investors also buy and sell the futures contracts in attempt to make a profit and provide liquidity to the system. However, due to the financial leverage provided to traders by the exchange, commodity futures traders face a substantial risk

Chapter 4

Technical Indicators for Commodities Investing

4.1 Introduction

The primary motive for any trader, investor or speculator is to make trading as profitable as possible. Primarily two techniques, fundamental analysis and technical analysis, are employed for making buy, sell or hold decisions. The technique of fundamental analysis is believed to be ideal for investments involving a longer time period. It is more research based; it studies demand-supply situations, economic policies, and financials as decision-making criteria.

Technical analysis is commonly used by traders, as it is appropriate for short term judgment in the markets--namely, deciding a quick buy and sell, entry and exit points, etc. It is pictorial; it analyzes the past price patterns, trends and volume to construct charts in order to determine future movement. These techniques can be used for trading all asset classes ranging from stocks to commodities. In this article, we will concentrate on commodities, which include things like cocoa, coffee, copper, corn, cotton, crude oil, feeder cattle, gold, heating oil, live cattle, lumber, natural gas, oats, orange juice, platinum, pork bellies, rough rice, silver, soybeans, sugar, etc.

The technical analyst will use a number of methods when reviewing commodity markets. These methods typically include such things as Price Action (pattern recognition, candle stick charts, Elliott Wave analysis, etc.), Seasonal Factors and Technical Indicators.

Given the nature of the question this response will focus on the latter.

When trading commodities, a technical analyst will most likely use the same indicators on a chart to predict the future as with many other instruments (e.g. equities). When looking at the big picture, charts that reflect long periods (e.g. weekly or monthly) should be used to assess the primary trends. Shorter period charts (e.g. daily) are used mainly to determine the entry and exit point of a trade.

Technical Indictors fall into different categories, but the Indicators that most technical analysts use are a measure of momentum.

Momentum Indicators, as the name suggests, measure the momentum behind the move. Just as a car will struggle to move forward without a foot on the accelerator, so too will a market struggle to move higher if momentum begins to falter. On the downside, once downward momentum begins to abate, the prospect of stability and a renewed upwards trend begin to improve.

Momentum Indicators fall into two broad categories, Trend Following and Oscillators. Trend Following Indicators include Moving Averages, Bollinger Bands and Moving Average Convergence/Divergence (MACD). Oscillators encompass such indicators as the Relative Strength Index (RSI) and the Stochastic.

Before applying any of the Indicators, the trader or investor needs to firstly identify the type of market; is it a ranging or trending market? This needs to be determined because Oscillators are ineffective in trending markets, and similarly, Trend Following indicators are misleading in ranging markets.

Oscillators register overbought and oversold market levels, and the problem with using them in trending markets is that they will move to overbought or oversold levels and stay there for quite some time. This will cause the trader to exit or enter prematurely. Conversely, Trend Following indicators will 'whipsaw' traders in a ranging market.

Therefore, when using Technical Indicators in the analysis of commodity markets, the first requirement is to identify the trend. Once the trend has been identified, the trader can then apply some of the commonly used Indicators mentioned above: Moving Averages, MACD, the RSI, the Stochastic and Bollinger Bands.

Let's take a look at each in turn:

4.2 Moving Averages

The simplest indicator one can use is the moving average. This can, for example, be the 9 and 20 day moving averages (MA). The analyst will study their cross-overs and the relative position of the price with respect to the moving averages. Prices movements on a chart can be shown in different formats such as bars, candles or lines. The cross-over between two moving averages may signal a change in trend. When the fast MA (9 day) crosses the slow MA (20 day) from below to above, it will signify a bullish trend. If it crosses from above to below, it will signify a bearish trend. Moving averages may in some situations be used as support or resistance levels for a given trade.

There are many versions of MA which are more elaborate like exponential moving average (EMA), volume adjusted moving average, linear weighted moving average, etc. MA is not suitable for a ranging market, as it tends to generate false signals due to prices moving back and forth. Remember, the slope of the MA reflects the direction of the trend. The steeper the MA, move is the momentum backing the trend, while a flattening MA is a warning signal as there might be a trend reversal due to reduction in momentum.

4.3 MACD

Another commonly used indicator is the MACD, which is an abbreviation for Moving Average Convergence Divergence. The MACD is a trend-following momentum indicator that measures the difference between two Exponential Moving Averages (EMA).

Simply put, when the MACD is rising it indicates that the 12 day EMA is trading above the 26 day EMA. This implies positive momentum. If this is above the 'trigger line' (the 9 day EMA) then the stock is considered bullish. If both lines are falling, the stock is under selling pressure.

The simplest interpretation of a bullish (bearish) moving average crossover occurs when MACD moves above (falls below) its 9-day EMA or 'trigger line'. If a market is trending down but the 'trigger line' rises above the MACD, this implies that downward momentum is decreasing and there is a good chance that a reversal is imminent.

A bullish signal is generated when the MACD is a positive value as the shorter period EMA is higher (stronger) than the longer period EMA. This signifies increase in upside momentum but as the value starts declining, it shows loss in momentum. Similarly, a negative MACD value is indicative of a bearish situation and if this tends to increase further it suggests a rise in downside momentum. If negative MACD value decreases, it signals that the down trend is losing its momentum. There are more interpretations to the movement of these lines like crossovers; a bullish crossover is signaled when the MACD crosses above the signal line in an upward direction.

4.4 The RSI

The Relative Strength Index (RSI) is used to identify when a market is overbought or oversold. It is computed by analyzing all the bullish ranges against all the bearish ranges during a particular period of time (usually 14 days). By adding all the bullish trades (when prices went up) and dividing it by the summation of the bearish days (when prices went down) we then turn it into an index from 0 to 100. A general rule is that when the RSI crosses the 30 line from below, it signifies a bullish signal and when it crosses the 70 line from above, it signifies a bearish signal.

4.5 Stochastic

This indicator is based on the observation that, as price is moving higher the closing price tends to be closer to the upper end of the day's price range. And when prices are falling, the closing price tends to gravitate to the lower end of the day's range.

The Stochastic is plotted as two lines called %K, a fast line and %D, a slow line. The most common time period for %K is 14 days, but like the RSI it is best to experiment to find what time period works best for a particular market. What %K measures on a scale of 0 to 100, is where today's close is relative to the total 14 day range. The %D line is a moving average of %K.

Readings above 80 are considered overbought and readings below 20 are considered oversold.

4.6 Bollinger Bands

The basis of these relate to the theory that a market's probable movements (up or down) can be traced to two standard deviations. This means that 90% of all price movements will be confined within a band around the mean. The latter is usually computed from a 20-day moving average and the bands are on either side of the mean. The bands will contract or expand as the price of the commodity oscillates within the bands. As the daily ranges approach the band on either side and exceed the band value, it may signify that a reversal is imminent.

4.7 Interpretations

With regard to the MACD, the RSI and the Stochastic, the above 'rules' are a very simplistic interpretation and will lead to many false signals. A better interpretation is to:

1. identify support and resistance levels;

2. define the 'signal line' and look for breaks above or below it; and
3. wait for divergences to develop from overbought or oversold levels.

Examples:

An example of using 'support and resistance' levels on an indicator

The study below shows the MACD breaking above the 'signal line' – which is a natural support/resistance level- in August 2004 (A). This confirmed the change in trend from Bearish to Bullish.

In September 2005 (B), the MACD moved back to test the support of the 'signal line', and bounced from it – thereby confirming that the trend was still positive. This occurred even as price had broken below a significant support level – thus the support on the indicator was more reliable than the price support.

In April 2007 (C) the MACD broke below the 'signal line' confirming the change from Bull to Bear.

Subsequently, the MACD was rejected from the signal line in December 2007(D). This gave an early warning that the rally from September was about to fail.

GOLD: A good example of the combination of two different indicators; Moving Averages (a 'trend following' indicator) and the Stochastic (an 'oscillator').

In late July, the gold price broke below the 9 and 20-day moving averages, and the Stochastic (an oscillator) turned down from overbought levels and broke below the 'signal line'. This combination registered a Sell signal.

However, note that the Stochastic pushed to overbought levels earlier in the year, and stayed there for an extended period. Thus taking an overbought reading as a signal to Sell is not, by itself, a good trading strategy. Price was still above rising moving averages at the time; confirming a rising trend – therefore an overbought level on the Stochastic was not a reliable indicator.

The trader will take this into consideration when assessing the outlook for a commodity.

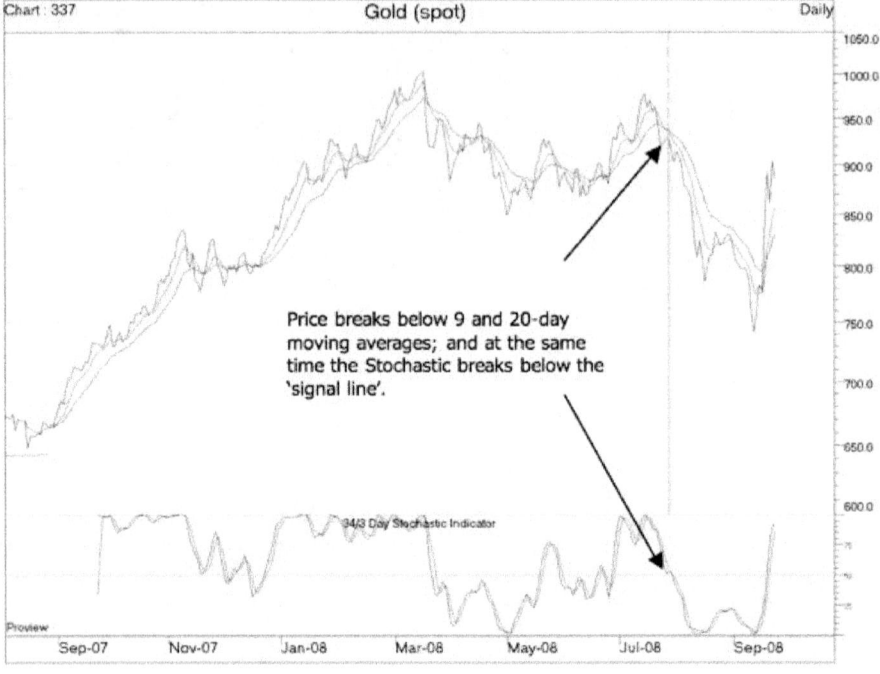

Chapter 5

Commodity futures and option

5.1 Introduction

An effective and efficient market for trading in commodities *futures requires:*

- *Volatility in the prices of the underlying commodities.*

- *Large numbers of buyers and sellers with diverse risk profiles(hedgers, speculators and arbitrageurs).*

- *The underlying physical commodities to be fungible, i.e. they should be exchangeable.*

5.2 Features of commodity futures

1. Organized:

Commodity Futures contracts always trade on an organized exchange, e.g. NCDEX, MCX, etc in India and NYMEX, LME, COMEX etc. internationally.

2. Standardized:

Commodity Futures contracts are highly standardized with the quality, quantity, and delivery date, being predetermined.

3. Eliminates Counterparty Risk:

Commodity Futures exchanges use clearing houses to guarantee that the terms of the futures contract are fulfilled. The Clearing House guarantees that the contract will be fulfilled, eliminating the risk of any default by the other party.

4. Facilitates Margin Trading:

Commodity Futures traders do not have to put up the entire value of a contract. Rather, they are required to post a margin that is roughly 4 to 8% of the total value of the contract (this margin varies across exchanges and commodities). This facilitates taking of leveraged positions.

5. Closing a Position:

Futures markets are closely regulated by government agencies, e.g. Forward Markets Commission (FMC) in India, Commodity Futures Trading Commission in (CFTC) USA, etc. This ensures fair practices in these markets.

6. Regulated Markets Environment:

Commodity Futures contracts are highly standardized with the quality, quantity, and delivery date, being predetermined.

7. Physical Delivery:

Actual delivery of the commodity can be made or taken on expiry of the contract. Physical delivery requires the member to provide the exchange with prior delivery information and completion of all the delivery related formalities as specified by the exchange.

5.3 Different types of market players

In order to understand the commodity market participants like hedgers, speculators and arbitrageurs, it is essential to first understand all the features, terms and conditions of the commodity futures contract.

in efficient market for commodity futures requires a large number of market participants with diverse risk profiles. Ownership of the underlying commodity is not required for trading in commodity futures. The market participants simply need to deposit sufficient money with brokerage firms to cover the margin requirements. Market participants can be broadly divided into hedgers, speculators and arbitrageurs.

A Hedgers:

Simply put, hedging is a kind of insurance for your portfolio. When people hedge, they are, in reality, insuring their investment against any unpredicted events. Hedging does not prevent such events, but reduces the impact they might otherwise have on your portfolio.

Portfolio managers, retail investors, corporations as well as governments use hedging to reduce their risk exposure. However, when it comes to trading in commodities, hedging is not as simple as paying your insurance premium. To offset the risk arising from one instrument, traders use other instruments.

They are generally the commercial producers and consumers of the traded commodities. They participate in the market to manage their spot market price risk. Commodity prices *are volatile and their participation in the futures market allows them to hedge or protect themselves against the risk of losses from fluctuating prices. For e.g. a copper smelter will hedge by selling copper futures, since it is exposed to the risk of falling copper prices.*

B Speculators:

A speculator is a person who trades derivatives, commodities, bonds, equities or currencies with a higher than average risk in return for a higher-than-average profit potential. Speculators take large risks, especially with respect to anticipating future price movements, in the hope of making quick, large gains.

Speculators usually try to catch and ride fast moving trends, so that they could project in what direction the market will go. In this case they use technical analysis methodology alongside analysis of fundamentals, as the latter could range from changing consumer sentiment, expectations, to fluctuating interest rates, retail sales or consumer spending indicators, consumer price and producer price indexes, gross domestic product for a country/region, or just a single public statement by experts, CEOs, Presidents of prestigious and internationally renowned corporations and institutions. Speculators are able to register large gains or equally huge losses and usually belong to the group of high net investors, who strive at diversification of their investment portfolios. They always pursue profit maximization within a short term.

They are traders who speculate on the direction of the futures prices with the intention of making money. Thus, for the speculators, trading in commodity futures is an investment option. Most Speculators do not prefer to make or accept deliveries of the actual commodities; rather they liquidate their positions before the expiry date of the contract.

C Arbitrageurs:

Arbitrageurs usually participate in an extremely rapid environment, with decisions being made at the blink of an eye, literally. Sometimes the price of a share in the spot market may be below or may exceed its price in the derivatives market. Arbitrageurs usually look to dispose of such imperfections and inefficiencies in the market. They also play a key role in increasing market's liquidity.

They are traders who buy and sell to make money on price differentials across different markets. Arbitrage involves simultaneous sale and purchase of the same commodities in different markets. Arbitrage keeps the prices in different markets in line with each other. Usually such transactions are risk free.

The market functions because of the differing risk profiles of the market participants. The fluctuation in commodity prices represents both, a risk and a potential for profit. The hedgers transfer this risk by foregoing the associated profit potential. The speculators assume this risk in the hope of realizing profits by predicting price movements. The arbitrageurs make the process of price discovery more efficient.

Once we understand what are the risks and returns involved for respective Commodity Market Participants, we can start investing in different commodity avenues.

In the next chapter we will learn about why commodity futures are good investment avenues along with it's advantages and different commodities traded in commodities market.

Some of the reasons that make investing in commodity futures an attractive preposition are described below:

·

D Leverage:

In finance, leverage (sometimes referred to as gearing in the United Kingdom and Australia) is any technique involving the use of borrowed funds in the purchase of an asset, with the expectation that the after tax income from the asset and asset

Commodity Futures trading is done on margins. The investor only deposits a fraction of the value of the futures contract with the broker to cover the exchange specified margin requirements. This gives the investor greater leverage and thus the ability to generate higher returns.

E Liquidity:

Unlike investment vehicles like real estate, investments in commodity futures offer high liquidity. It is equally easy to both buy and sell futures and an investor can easily liquidate his position whenever required. There is also another advantage of being able to use the profits from a trade elsewhere, without having to close the position.

F Diversification:

Investments in commodity markets are an excellent means of portfolio diversification. For example, gold prices have historically shown a low correlation with most other asset prices (such as equities) and thus offer an excellent means for portfolio diversification.

G Inflation Hedge:

As the commodity prices determine price levels and consequently inflation, investing in commodity futures can act as a hedge against inflation.

H Physical Gold:

Physical Gold is a product by which retail and high net worth investors can take investment positions in dematerialized physical gold using the futures market. In this product, the investor can hold physical gold, in a safe deposit vault approved by the exchange, which is reflected in the investor's demat account. The main features of this are:

- Liquidity

- • ▪ Assurance of purity
- • ▪ Transparency of rates
- • ▪ Safety

These features have attracted a large number of clients to the product since its introduction. Many brokers offer a full package of services associated with the Physical Gold contract, including acting as commission agent to take care of sales tax / VAT related issues.

5.4 Basis Defined

The difference between the local spot price (cash price) and the relevant futures price of a commodity is called the commodity basis.

Basis = Spot price - Futures price

For example, if the spot landed price of gold in March is Rs. 9450/10gm and the April gold futures price is Rs. 9400/10gm, then the basis is Rs. 50/10gm (9450-9400). The basis can be positive or negative.

The spot price of a commodity is the prevailing cash price in the market. The futures price is a representation of the market opinion of the spot price of the commodity on some future date. Theoretically, the futures price and the spot price are related in the following manner

Futures price = Spot price + Cost of carry

The cost of carry is the cost of carrying the commodity from the current month to the month of delivery. This includes costs of storage, insurance, interest etc. Thus usually, the price of a futures contract is higher than the prevailing spot price. This condition is known as Contango.

The actual difference between the spot and the futures price may be different from the cost of carry and can vary based on the demand and supply of the underlying commodity at current and expected levels in the future. Thus it is possible for the futures price to be less than the spot price. This condition is called Backwardation. For e.g. the copper futures on NYMEX have mostly been in backwardation since the 1950's.

Whether the market is in Contango or Backwardation, as the futures contract approaches the expiry date, the spot and future prices converge.

Spot Price < Futures Price	Basis	Market Condition
	Negative	Canting or Normal

Spot Price < Futures Price	Basis	Market Condition
	Positive	Backwardation or Abnormal

The basis depends on the local spot market price and so it reflects the local market conditions. It is affected by the following factors:

- Local supply and demand.
- Storage costs.
- Profit margins.

Basis is usually a negative number because of carrying charges. In normal market conditions, cash prices are lower than the nearby futures prices. With the approach of delivery on the futures, carrying charges diminish and the price difference between cash and futures will decrease.

It is important to understand Commodity Futures Basis, Spot Price, Futures Price and the relation between Weakening Basis and Strengthening Basis as these are the key metrics that will help you to take better Commodity Trading Decisions.

asis is a crucial factor on which hedging decisions are based. The matrix of sale and purchase for producers and consumers on basis is given below:

Long Hedge	**High Cash Price**	**Low Cash Price**
Strong Basis	Delay Cash Purchase No Hedging Required	• Delay Cash Purchase • Hedge - Long Futures
Weak Basis	Purchase immediate requirements only	Purchase as much as possible and store or Hedge using futures

Short Hedge	**High Cash Price**	**Low Cash Price**
Strong Basis	Sell Product in Cash	• Sell Produce • Re-own by going long on futures
Weak Basis	• Delay Cash Sales / Store Produce • Hedge - Short Futures	Store for selling later

The long hedger or the consumer of the commodity prefers for the basis to weaken. In this scenario, the cash price will be lower than futures and hence the hedger's procurement price in the spot market will be less than the futures market.

The short hedger or the producer of the commodity prefers for the basis to strengthen. In this scenario the cash price will be higher relative to the future and the hedger realizes a higher selling price in the spot market than the futures market.

5.5 Call options

In a call option counterparties enter into a financial contract option where the buyer p*urchases the right but not the obligation to buy an agreed quantity of a particular commodity or financial instrument (the underlying) from the seller of the option at a certain time (the expiration date) for a certain price (the* strike *price). The seller (or "writer") is obligated to sell the commodity or financial instrument should the buyer so decide. The buyer pays a fee (called a premium) for this right*

n traditional *stock market exchanges such as the New York Stock Exchange (NYSE), most trading activity took place in the trading pits in face-to-face interactions between brokers and dealers in open outcry trading. In 1992 the Financial Information exchange (FIX) protocol was introduced, allowing international real-time exchange of information regarding market transactions. The U.S. Securities and Exchange Commission ordered U.S. stock markets to convert from the fractional system to a decimal system by April 2001. Metrification, conversion from the imperial system of measurement to the metrical, increased throughout the 20th century. Eventually FIX-compliant interfaces were adopted globally by commodity exchanges using the FIX Protocol In 2001 the Chicago Board of Trade and the Chicago Mercantile Exchange (later merged into the CME group, the world's largest futures exchange company) launched their FIX-compliant interface.*

By 2011, the alternative trading system (ATS) of electronic trading featured computers buying and selling without human dealer intermediation. High-frequency trading (HFT) algorithmic trading, had almost phased out "dinosaur floor-traders".

5.6 Derivatives

Derivatives *evolved from simple commodity future contracts into a diverse group of financial instruments that apply to every kind of asset, including mortgages, insurance and many more. Futures contracts, Swaps (1970s-), Exchange-traded Commodities (ETC) (2003-), forward contracts, etc. are examples. They can be traded through formal exchanges or through Over-the-counter (OTC). Commodity market derivatives unlike credit default derivatives for example, are secured by the physical assets or commodities.*

5.7 Forward contracts

A forward contract is *an agreement between two parties to exchange at some fixed future date a given quantity of a commodity for a price defined when the contract is finalized. The fixed price is known as the forward price. Such forward contracts began as a way of reducing pricing risk in food and agricultural product markets, because farmers knew what price they would receive for their output.*

Forward contracts for example, were used for rice in seventeenth century Japan.

Futures contract

Contracts are standardized forward contracts that are transacted through an exchange. In futures contracts the buyer and the seller stipulate product, grade, quantity and location and leaving price as the only variable.[

Agricultural futures contracts are the oldest, in use in the United States for more than 170 years. Modern futures agreements, began in Chicago in the 1840s, with the appearance of the railroads. Chicago, centrally located, emerged as the hub between MidwFutures estern farmers and east coast consumer population centers.

Swaps

A Swap *is a derivative in which counterparties exchange the cash flows of one party's financial instrument for those of the other party's financial instrument. They were introduced in the 1970s.*

Chapter 6

Top traded commodities

6.1

The top traded commodities in the world are as follows

Top traded commodities

Rank	Commodity	Value in US$ ('000)	Date of information
1	Mineral fuels, oils, distillation products, etc.	$3,183,079,941	2015
2	Electrical, electronic equipment	$2,833,534,414	2015
3	Machinery, nuclear reactors, boilers, etc.	$2,763,371,813	2015
4	Vehicles other than railway, tramway	$1,876,830,856	2015
5	Plastics and articles thereof	$770,226,676	2015
6	Optical, photo, technical, medical, etc. apparatus	$665,101,524	2015
7	Pharmaceutical products	$543,596,577	2015
8	Iron and steel	$479,113,147	2015
9	Organic chemicals	$397,462,088	2015

Top traded commodities

Rank	Commodity	Value in US$ ('000)	Date of information
10	Pearls, precious stones, metals, coins, etc.	$368,155,369	2015

6.2 Energy

Energy commodities include crude oil particularly WTI) crude oil and Brent crude oil, natural gas, Hedging is a coFor many years, West Texas Intermediate (WTI) crude oil, a light, sweet crude oil, was the world's most-traded commodity. WTI is a grade used as a benchmark in oil pricing. It is the underlying commodity of Chicago Mercantile Exchange's oil futures contracts. WTI is often referenced in news reports on oil prices, alongside Brent Crude. WTI is lighter and sweeter than Brent and considerably lighter and sweeter than Dubai or Oman.

From April through October 2012, Brent futures contracts exceeded those for WTI, the longest streak since at least 1995.[

Crude oil can be light or heavy. Oil was the first form of energy to be widely traded. Some commodity market speculation is directly related to the stability of certain states, e.g., Iraq, Bahrain, Iran, Venezuela and many others. Most commodities markets are not so tied to the politics of volatile regions.

Oil and gasoline are traded in units of 1,000 barrels (42,000 US gallons). WTI crude oil is traded through NYMEX under trading symbol CL and through Intercontinental Exchange (ICE) under trading symbol WTI. Brent crude oil is traded in through Intercontinental Exchange under trading symbol B. Gulf Coast Gasoline is traded through NYMEX with the trading symbol of LR. Gasoline (reformulated gasoline blendstock for oxygen blending or RBOB) is traded through NYMEX via trading symbol

RB. Propane is traded through NYMEX, a subsidiary of Intercontinental Exchange since early 2013, via trading symbol PN.

Natural gas is traded through NYMEX a subsidiary of Intercontinental Exchange in units of 10,000 mmBTU with the trading symbol of NG. Heating oil is traded through NYMEX, a subsidiary of Intercontinental Exchange, under trading symbol HO.

Crude Oil

Overview

Crude oil is a naturally occurring, unrefined petroleum product composed of hydrocarbon deposits in natural underground pools or reservoirs and remains liquid at atmospheric pressure and temperature. Although it is often called "black gold," crude oil has a wide ranging viscosity and can vary in colour to various shades of black and yellow depending on its hydrocarbon composition. Crude oil can be refined to produce usable products such as gasoline, diesel and various forms of petrochemicals.

Even though most crude oil is produced by a relatively small number of companies, and often located in remote locations far from the point of consumption, trading in crude oil on a global basis has always been robust. Nearly 80% of international crude oil is transported through waterways in large tankers and most of the rest by inland pipelines

The majority of oil reserves in the world is in the Middle East, at 48 per cent of the known and identified reserves. This is followed by North America, Africa, Central and South America, Eurasia, Asia and Oceania, and Europe.

OPEC controls almost 40 per cent of the world's crude oil, accounts for about 75 per cent of the world's proven oil reserves, and exports 55 per cent of the oil traded internationally.

In oil trading, risk management techniques are extremely important for the various stakeholders and participants, such as producers, exporters, marketers, processors, and SMEs. Modern techniques and strategies, including market-based risk management financial instruments like Crude Oil Futures, offered on the MCX platform can improve efficiencies and consolidate competitiveness through price risk management.

Factors Influencing the Market

- OPEC output or supply
- Changing scenarios in oil demand from emerging and developing countries
- US crude and products inventories
- Refinery Utilization rate
- Global geopolitics
- Speculative buying and selling
- Weather conditions

6.3 Metals

Precious metals

Precious metals currently traded on the commodity market include gold, platinum, and silver which are sold by the COMEX. troy ounce. One of the main exchanges for these precious metals is

According to the World Gold Council, investments in gold are the primary driver of industry growth. Gold prices are highly volatile, driven by large flows of speculative money.[

Gold

Gold is the oldest precious metal known to man and for thousands of years it has been valued as a global currency, a commodity, an investment and simply an object of beauty.

Overview

- Gold, the most sought-after of all precious metals, is acquired throughout the world for its beauty, liquidity, investment qualities, and industrial properties. As an investment vehicle, gold is typically viewed as a financial asset that maintains its value and purchasing power during inflationary periods.

- Gold has a long and fascinating usage history in a diverse range of industries and applications. In each of the applications it is used, gold provides an outstanding performance due to its unique properties of being one of the most malleable and ductile metals with high melting point and easy recyclability. Gold is a material of choice in medicine and dentistry as it is biocompatible. In recent years it has emerged as a key nonmaterial. Global demand for gold is centered on four primary categories: jeweler, investment, central bank reserves, and technology.

- Risk management is of critical importance for gold value chain participants, such as mining companies, processors, companies dealing in gold and gold products, jewellers, and even governments which rely on the proceeds of bullion consumption and trade. Modern hedging techniques and strategies, including market-based risk management financial instruments, such as gold futures, can improve efficiencies and consolidate competitiveness.

Factors Influencing the Market

1 Above-ground supply of gold from central bank sales, reclaimed scrap, and official gold loans.

2 Hedging interest of producers and miners.

3 World macroeconomic factors, such as movement in the dollar and interest rate, and economic events.

In India, gold demand is also influenced by seasonality, that is, marriage and harvesting.

Silver

Overview

- Silver is a brilliant grey-white metal that is soft and malleable. The mining of silver began some 5000 years ago, with the first mine being in Anatolia (modern-day Turkey). The principal sources of silver are the ores of silver, silver-nickel, lead, and lead-zinc obtained from Peru, Bolivia, Mexico, China, Australia, Chile, Poland, and Serbia. Peru, Bolivia, and Mexico have been mining silver since 1546, and are still major world producers. Just over half of the mined silver comes from Mexico, Peru, China, and Australia, the four largest producing countries. Primary mines produce about one-third of the world silver, while around two-thirds come as a by-product of gold, copper, lead, and zinc mining. The top three silver-producing mines are Cannington

(Australia), Fresnillo (Mexico), and San Cristobal (Bolivia). In Central Asia, Tajikistan is known to have some of the largest silver deposits in the world.

- Silver has innumerable applications in art, science, industry and beyond. At the highest level, though, demand for silver breaks down into three important categories: silver in industry, investment, and silver jewellery and décor. Together, these three areas represent more than 95% of the annual silver demand. With unique properties, including its strength, malleability, and ductility; its electrical and thermal conductivity; its sensitivity to and high reflectance of light; and the ability to endure extreme temperature; it is an element without substitution. Commercial-grade fine silver is at least 99.9% pure, and purities greater than 99.999% are available.

Factors Influencing the Market

- Economic events such as India's industrial growth, the global financial crisis, recession, and inflation affect prices.
- Geopolitical events involving governments or economic paradigms and armed conflict can cause major changes.
- Commodity-specific events, such as the construction of new production facilities, introduction of new processes, unexpected mine or plant closures, and industry restructuring, too affect the market.

6.4 Industrial metals

Industrial metals are sold by the metric ton through the London Metal Exchange and New York Mercantile Exchange. The London Metal Exchange trades include copper, aluminum, lead, tin, aluminum alloy, nickel, cobalt and molybdenum. In 2007, steel began trading on the London Metal Exchange.

Iron ore has been the latest addition to industrial metal derivatives. Deutsche Bank first began offering iron ore swaps in 2008, other banks quickly followed. Since then the size of the market has more than doubled each year between 2008 and 2012.

A **hedge** is an investment position intended to offset potential losses or gains that may be incurred by a companion investment. In simple language, a hedge is used to reduce any substantial losses or gains suffered by an individual or an organization.

A hedge can be constructed from many types of financial instruments, including stocks, exchange-traded funds, insurance, forward contracts, swaps, options, gamblesmany types of over-the-counter and derivative products, and futures contracts.

Public futures markets were established in the 19th century to allow transparent, standardized, and efficient hedging of agricultural commodity prices; they have since expanded to include futures contracts for hedging the values of energy, precious metals, foreign currency, and interest rate fluctuations.

Copper

Overview

In world metal consumption, copper ranks third after steel and aluminum. It is a product whose fortunes directly reflect the state of the world's economy, hence also dubbed as Dr Copper.

Copper, the best non-precious metal conductor of electricity, has exceptional strength, ductility, and resistance to creeping and corrosion to make it the preferred and safest conductor of electrical wiring in buildings. Economic, technological, and societal factors influence the supply and demand of copper. Land-based resources are estimated at 1.6 billion tonnes of copper, and resources in deep-sea nodules are estimated at 0.7 billion tonnes. Worldwide, approximately one-third of all copper consumed is recycled copper.

Copper is produced in more than 25 countries today. Because of global dispersion of copper production, the risk of disruption in global supplies is low. On the other hand, because of its importance in construction and power transmission, any disruption in supplies will have a major effect on the economy.

Producers, exporters, marketers, processors, and SMEs with exposure to copper can manage their price risks by hedging. When uncertainty looms large, modern risk management techniques and strategies, including market-based risk management financial instruments like 'Copper Futures', offered on the MCX platform can improve efficiencies and consolidate competitiveness through price risk management. The importance of risk management thus cannot be overstated.

Factors Influencing the Market

- copper prices reflect prevailing international spot market and the USD–INR exchange rates.

- Commodity-specific events, such as the construction of new production facilities or processes, new uses or the discontinuance of historical uses, unexpected mine or plant closures (natural disaster, supply disruption, accident, strike, and so forth), or industry restructuring—all affect the price of the metal.

- *Trade policies set by the government (implementation or suspension of taxes, penalties and quotas) affect supplies as they regulate (restricting or encouraging) material flow.*

Overview

- *Aluminum is a chemical element in the boron group with symbol Al and is the most widely used non-ferrous metal. Ancient Greeks and Romans used aluminum salts as dyeing mordents and as astringents for dressing wounds. It is a silvery white, soft, ductile metal. It makes up about 8% by weight of the earth's solid surface and after oxygen and silicon, the third most abundant of all elements in the earth's crust. Because of its strong affinity to oxygen, it is not found in the elemental state but only in combined forms, such as oxides or silicates. The metal derives its name from alumen, the Latin name for alum.*

- *Aluminum is theoretically 100% recyclable without any loss of its natural qualities. According to the International Resource Panel's Metal Stocks in Society report, the global per capita stock of aluminum in use in society (that is in cars, buildings and electronics) is 80 kg. Much of this is in more developed countries (350 kg–500 kg per capita) rather than in less-developed countries (35 kg per capita). Knowing the per capita stocks and their approximate lifespan is important for planning recycling. By consumption, aluminum is next to steel.*

- *The realities of the market call for risk management techniques that are critical for users of aluminum, such as producers, exporters, marketers, processors, and SMEs. When uncertainty looms large, modern techniques and strategies, including market-based risk management financial instruments like 'Aluminum Futures', offered on the MCX platform can improve efficiencies and consolidate competitiveness through price risk management. The importance of risk management thus cannot be overstated.*

Factors Influencing the Market

- Prices ruling in the international markets
- Indian rupee and US dollar exchange rates
- Economic factors: industrial growth, global financial crisis, recession, and inflation
- Commodity-specific events: construction of new production facilities or processes, new uses or the discontinuance of historical uses, unexpected mine or plant closures (natural disaster, supply disruption, accident, strike, and so forth), and industry restructuring
- Government trade policies (implementation or suspension of taxes, penalties, and quotas)
- Geopolitical events

Zinc

Overview

- Zinc is the fourth most widely used metal in the world after steel, aluminium, and copper. It is hard and brittle at most temperatures, but becomes malleable between 100 °C and 150 °C. It is a fair conductor of heat and electricity and burns with a bright bluish-green flame, giving off zinc oxide fumes. Zinc occurs naturally in the earth's crust and is the 24th most abundant element, with about 1.9 billion tonnes of identified resources. It is an essential trace element and necessary for plants, animals, and microorganisms. However, high levels of zinc exposure through inhalation, ingestion, and dermal contact could cause adverse health effects.

- Due to its resistance to non-acidic atmospheric corrosion, zinc plays a vital role in extending the life of buildings, vehicles, ships, and so on. The metal is mainly used as an anti-corrosion agent, and a coat of zinc prevents rusting of galvanized steel. It also finds its use in the automobile, battery, petroleum, paint, fungicide, rubber, and chemical industries—a few among the many industrial uses it is being put to today.

- Stakeholders of the zinc market consisting among others, producers, exporters, marketers, processors, and SMEs, can use modern risk management techniques and strategies, including market-based risk management financial instruments like Zinc Futures, offered on the MCX platform to improve efficiencies and consolidate competitiveness.

Factors Influencing the Market

- Zinc prices in India are fixed based on the rates that rule in the international spot market, and INR–USD exchange rates.

- Economic events, such as the national industrial growth, global financial crisis, recession, and inflation, affect metal prices.

- As societies develop, their demand for metal increases based on their current economic position, which could also be referred to as 'national economic growth factor'.

6.5 Agricultural commodity price hedging

A typical hedger might be a commercial farmer. The market values of wheat and other crops fluctuate constantly as supply and demand for them vary, with occasional large moves in either direction. Based on current prices and forecast levels at harvest time, the farmer might decide that planting wheat is a good idea one season, but the price of wheat might change over time. Once the farmer plants wheat, he is committed to it for an entire growing season. If the actual price of wheat rises greatly between planting and harvest, the farmer stands to make a lot of unexpected money, but if the actual price drops by harvest time, he is going to lose the invested money.

Because the uncertainty of future supply and demand fluctuations and the price risk imposed on the farmer, they will use different financial transactions to reduce, or hedge, their risk. One such transaction is the use of forward contracts. Forward contracts are mutual agreements to deliver a certain amount of a commodity at a certain date for a specified price and each contract is unique to the buyer and seller. For this example, the farmer can sell a number of forward contracts equivalent to the amount of wheat he expects to harvest and essentially lock in the current price of wheat. Once the forward contracts expire, the farmer will harvest the wheat and deliver it to the buyer at the price agreed to in the forward contract. Therefore, the farmer has reduced his risks to fluctuations in the market of wheat because he has already guaranteed a certain number of bushels for a certain price. However, there are still many risks associated with this type of hedge. For example, if the farmer has a low yield year and he harvests less than the amount specified in the forward contracts, he must purchase the bushels elsewhere in order to fill the contract. This becomes even more of a problem when the lower yields affect the entire wheat industry and the price of wheat increases due to supply and demand pressures. Also, while the farmer hedged all of the risks of a price decrease away by locking in the price with a forward contract, he also gives up the right to the benefits of a price increase. Another risk associated with the forward contract is the risk of default or renegotiation. The forward contract locks in a certain amount and price at a certain future date. Because of that, there is always the possibility that the buyer will not pay the amount required at the end of the contract or that the buyer will try to renegotiate the contract before it expires.

Future contracts are another way our farmer can hedge his risk without a few of the risks that forward contracts have. Future contracts are similar to forward contracts except they are more standardized (i.e. each contract is the same quantity and date for everyone). These contracts trade on exchanges and are guaranteed through clearinghouses. Clearinghouses ensure that every contract is honored and they take the opposite side of every contract. Future contracts typically are more liquid than forward contracts and move with the market. Because of this, the farmer can minimize the risk he faces in the future through the selling of future contracts. Future contracts also differ from forward contracts in that delivery never happens. The exchanges and clearinghouses allow the buyer or seller to leave the contract early and cash out. So tying back into the farmer selling his wheat at a future date, he will sell short futures contracts for the amount that he predicts to harvest to protect against a price decrease. The current (spot) price of wheat and the price of the futures contracts for wheat converge as time gets closer to the delivery date, so in order to make money on the hedge, the farmer must close out his position earlier than then. On the chance that prices decrease in the future, the farmer will make a profit on his short position in the futures market which offsets any decrease in revenues from the spot market for wheat. On the other hand, if prices increase, the farmer will generate a loss on the futures market which is offset by an increase in revenues on the spot market for wheat. Instead of agreeing to sell his wheat to one person on a set date, the farmer will just buy and sell futures on an exchange and then sell his wheat wherever he wants once he harvests

6.6 Fuel Hedging

Fuel Hedging is a contractual tool some large fuel consuming companies, such as airlines, cruise lines and trucking companies, use to reduce their exposure to volatile and potentially rising fuel costs. A fuel hedge contract allows a fuel-consuming company to establish a fixed or capped cost, via a commodity swap or option. The companies enter into hedging contracts to mitigate their exposure to future fuel prices that may be higher than current prices and/or to establish a known fuel cost for budgeting purposes. If such a company buys a fuel swap and the price of fuel declines, the company will effectively be forced to pay an above-market rate for fuel. If the company buys a fuel call option and the price of fuel increases, the company will receive a return on the option that offsets their actual cost of fuel. If the company buys a fuel call option, which requires an upfront premium cost, much like insurance, and the price of fuel decreases, the company will not receive a return on the option but they will benefit from buying fuel at the then-lower cost.

he cost of fuel hedging depends on the predicted future price of fuel. Airlines may place hedges either based on future prices of jet fuel or on future prices of crude oil. Because crude oil is the source of jet fuel, the prices of crude oil and jet fuel are normally correlated. However, other factors, such as difficulties regarding refinery capacity, may cause unusual divergence in the trends of crude oil and jet fuel.

Companies which consume large volumes of fuel and do not hedge their fuel costs generally believes one, if not both, of the following: 1. The company has the ability to pass on any and all increases in fuel prices to their customers, without a negative impact on their profit margins. 2. The company is confident that fuel prices are going to fall and is comfortable paying a higher price for fuel if, in fact, their analysis proves to be incorrect.

Typically, airlines will hedge only a certain portion of their fuel requirements for a certain period. Often, contracts for portions of an airline's jet fuel needs will overlap, with different levels of hedging expiring over time.

During the 2009-2010 period, the studies for the airline industry have shown the average hedging ratio to be 64%. Especially during the peak stress periods, the ratio tends to increase.

Southwest Airlines has tended to hedge a greater portion of its fuel needs as compared to other major U.S. domestic carriers Southwest's aggressive fuel hedging has helped the airline partially avoid financial consequences caused by airline industry downturns (e.g., the downturn caused by the 2000s energy crisis). Between 1999 and 2008, Southwest saved more than $4 billion through fuel hedging under the strategic leadership of former CFO Kelly (who became CEO in 2004, and President and Chairman in 2008).

Overview

MCX Training is your source of information on commodity derivatives training. Being the premier commodity exchange in India, MCX contributes towards transferring of knowledge to both internal and external recipients through its training programmers. The training cell performs a special role in the enlargement of human capital development across India by conducting training programmers in the commodity futures space, and offering courses in the learning and distance learning modes.

The programmers offered aim to improve skills, enabling participants to fulfill their potential within their respective organization. Moreover, the programmers are focused on those who want to be acquainted with the commodity derivatives markets and emphasize on the modalities of risk management, operations, clearing & settlement, and regulations among others.

Chapter 7

Terminology

Arbitrage - *The simultaneous purchase and sale of similar commodities in different markets to take advantage of a price discrepancy.*

- **Arbitration** - *The procedure of settling disputes between members, or between members and customers.*

- **Bar Chart** - *A chart that show graphs the high, low, and settlement prices for a specific trading session over a given period of time.*

- **Basis** - *The difference between the current cash price and the futures price of the same commodity. Unless otherwise specified, the price of the nearby futures contract month is generally used to calculate the basis.*

- **Bear** - *Someone who thinks market prices will decline downward.*

- **Bear Market** - *A period of declining market prices.*

- **Bid** - *An expression indicating a desire to buy a commodity at a given price; opposite of offer.*

- **Broker** - *A company or individual that executes futures and options orders on behalf of financial and commercial institutions and/or the general public.*

- **Brokerage Fee** - *See Commission Fee.*

- **Brokerage House** - See Futures Commission Merchant.

- **Bull** - Someone who thinks market prices will rise.

- **Bull Market** - A period of rising market prices.

- **Carrying Charge** - For physical commodities such as grains and metals, the cost of storage space, insurance, and finance charges incurred by holding a physical commodity. Also referred to as cost of carry or carry.

- **Cash Commodity** - An actual physical commodity someone is buying or selling, e.g., soybeans, palm oil, gold, silver, etc. Also referred to as actuals.

- **Cash Market** - A place where people buy and sell the actual commodities. Also called spot market.

- **Charting** - The use of charts to analyze market behavior and anticipate future price movements. Those who use charting as a trading method plot such factors as high, low, and settlement prices; average price movements; volume; and open interest. Two basic price charts are bar charts and point-and-figure charts.

- **Clearing Corporation** - An independent corporation that settles all trades made at an exchange acting as a guarantor for all trades cleared by it, reconciles all clearing member firm accounts each day to ensure that all gains have been credited and all losses have been collected, and sets and adjusts clearing member firm margins for changing market conditions.

- **Clearing House** - An agency or separate corporation of a futures exchange that is responsible for settling trading accounts, clearing trades, collecting and maintaining margin monies, regulating delivery, and reporting trading data. Clearing houses act as third parties to all futures and options contracts acting as a buyer to every clearing member seller and a seller to every clearing member buyer.

- **Clearing Member** - A member of an exchange clearing house. by companies. Clearing members are responsible for the financial commitments of customers that clear through their firm.

- **Closing Price** - See Settlement Price.

- **Closing Range** - A range of prices at which buy and sell transactions took place during the market close.

- **Commission Fee** - A fee charged by a broker for executing a transaction. Also referred to as brokerage fee.

- **Commodity** - An article of commerce or a product that can be used for commerce. In a narrow sense, products traded on an authorized commodity exchange. The types of commodities include agricultural products, base metals, bullion and energy products.

- **Convergence** - A term referring to cash and futures prices tending to come together (i.e., the basis approaches zero) as the futures contract nears expiration.

- **Cost of Carry (or Carry)** - See Carrying Charge.

Daily Trading Limit - The maximum price range set by the exchange each day for a contract.

- **Deferred (Delivery) Month** - The more distant month(s) in which futures trading is taking place, as distinguished from the nearby (delivery) month.

- **Day Traders** - Speculators who take positions in futures and liquidate them prior to the close of the same trading day.

- **Deliverable Grades** - The standard grades of commodities or instruments listed in the rules of the exchanges that must be met when delivering cash commodities against futures contracts. Grades are often accompanied by a schedule of discounts and premiums allowable for delivery of commodities of lesser or greater quality than the standard called for by the exchange. Also referred to as contract grades.

- **Delivery** - The transfer of the cash commodity from the seller of a futures contract to the buyer of a futures contract. Each futures exchange has specific procedures for delivery of a cash commodity. Some futures contracts, such as stock index contracts, are cash settled.

- **Delivery Month** - A specific month in which delivery may take place under the terms of a futures contract. Also referred to as contract month.

- **Equilibrium Price** - The market price at which the quantity supplied of a commodity equals the quantity demanded.

- **Expiration Date** - Options on futures generally expire on a specific date during the month preceding the futures contract.

- **Full Carrying Charge Market** - A futures market where the price difference between delivery months reflects the total costs of interest, insurance, and storage.

- **Fundamental Analysis** - A method of anticipating future price movement using supply and demand information.

- **Futures Contract** - A legally binding agreement, made on the trading floor of a futures exchange, to buy or sell a commodity or financial instrument sometime in the future. Futures contracts are standardized according to the quality, quantity, and delivery time and location for each commodity. The only variable is price, which is discovered on an exchange-trading floor.

- **Futures Exchange** - A central marketplace with established rules and regulations where buyers and sellers meet to trade futures and options on futures contracts.

- **Hedger** - An individual or company owning or planning to own a cash commodity such as gold, soybeans, silver, etc. and concerned that the cost of the commodity may change. While holding it a hedger achieves protection against changing cash prices by purchasing (selling) futures contracts of the same or similar commodity.

- **Hedging** - The practice of offsetting the price risk inherent in any cash market position by taking an equal but opposite position in the futures market. Hedgers use the futures markets to protect their businesses from adverse price changes. See Selling (Short) Hedge and Purchasing (Long) Hedge.

- **High** - The highest price of the day for a particular futures contract.

- **Initial Margin** - The amount a futures market participant must deposit into his margin account at the time he places an order to buy (sell) a futures contract.

- **Inverted Market** - A futures market in which the more distant the contract month, the lower is the futures price.

- **Liquidate** - Selling (or purchasing) futures contracts of the same delivery month purchased (or sold) during an earlier transaction or making (or taking) delivery of the cash commodity represented by the futures contract. See Offset.

- **Long** - One who has bought futures contracts or owns a cash commodity.

- **Long Hedge** - Buying futures contracts to protect against a possible price increase of cash commodities that will be purchased in the future. At the time the cash commodities are bought, selling an equal number and type of futures contracts as those that were initially purchased closes the open futures position.

- **Low** - The lowest price of the day for a particular futures contract.

- **Maintenance Margin** - A set minimum margin (per outstanding futures contract) that a customer must maintain in his margin account.

- **Margin Call** - A call from a clearing house to a clearing member, or from a brokerage firm to a customer, to bring margin deposits up to a required minimum level.

- **Market Order** - An order to buy or sell a futures contract of a given delivery month to be filled at the best possible price and as soon as possible.

- **Marking-to-Market** - To debit or credit on a daily basis a margin account based on the close of that day's trading session. In this way, buyers and sellers are protected against the possibility of contract default.

Nearby (Delivery) Month - The futures contract month closest to expiration. Also referred to as spot month.

- **Offer** - An expression indicating one's desire to sell a commodity at a given price; opposite of bid.

- **Offset** - Taking a second futures position opposite to the initial or opening position. See Liquidate.

- **Open Interest** - The total number of futures contracts of a given commodity that have not yet been offset by an opposite futures transaction nor fulfilled by delivery of the commodity or option exercise. Each open transaction has a buyer and a seller, but for calculation of open interest, only one side of the contract is counted.

- **Position** - A market commitment. A buyer of a futures contract is said to have a long position and, conversely, a seller of futures contracts is said to have a short position.

- **Price Discovery** - The generation of information about "future" cash market prices through the futures markets.

- **Price Limit** - The maximum advance or decline from the previous day's settlement price permitted for a contract in one trading session by the rules of the exchange.

- **Settlement Close Out Price** - The last price paid for a commodity on any trading day. The exchange clearing house determines a firm's net gains or losses, margin requirements, and the next day's price limits, based on each futures and options contract settlement price. If there is a closing range of prices, the settlement close out price is determined by averaging those prices.

- **Short** - One who has sold futures contracts or plans to purchase a cash commodity. Selling futures contracts or initiating a cash forward contract sale without offsetting a particular market position.

- **Short Hedge** - Selling futures contracts to protect against possible declining prices of commodities that will be sold in the future. At the time the cash commodities are sold, purchasing an equal number and type of futures contracts as those that were initially sold closes the open futures position.

- **Speculator** - A market participant who tries to profit from buying and selling futures and options contracts by anticipating future price movements. Speculators assume market price risk and add liquidity and capital to the futures markets.

- **Spot** - Usually refers to a cash market price for a physical commodity that is available for immediate delivery.

- **Spread** - The price difference between two related markets or commodities or between contracts of different maturities of same commodity.

- **Volatility** - A measure of the change in price over a given time period. It is often expressed as a percentage and computed as the annualized standard deviation of percentage change in daily price.

- **Volume** - The number of purchases or sales of a commodity futures contract made during a specified period of time, often the total transactions for one trading day.

- ***Warehouse Receipt*** - *Document guaranteeing the existence and availability of a given quantity and quality of a commodity in storage; commonly used as the instrument of transfer of ownership in both cash and futures transactions.*

www.ingramcontent.com/pod-product-compliance
Lightning Source LLC
Chambersburg PA
CBHW061203180526
45170CB00002B/938